ISBN 978-0-243-13266-9
PIBN 10727001

1 MONTH OF
FREE
READING

at

www.ForgottenBooks.com

By purchasing this book you are eligible for one month membership to ForgottenBooks.com, giving you unlimited access to our entire collection of over 1,000,000 titles via our web site and mobile apps.

To claim your free month visit:

www.forgottenbooks.com/free78800

ISBN 978-0-365-20987-4
PIBN 10078800

English
Français
Deutsche
Italiano
Español
Português

www.forgottenbooks.com

Mythology Photography **Fiction**
Fishing Christianity **Art** Cooking
Essays Buddhism Freemasonry
Medicine **Biology** Music **Ancient
Egypt** Evolution Carpentry Physics
Dance Geology **Mathematics** Fitness
Shakespeare **Folklore** Yoga Marketing
Confidence Immortality Biographies
Poetry **Psychology** Witchcraft
Electronics Chemistry History **Law**
Accounting **Philosophy** Anthropology
Alchemy Drama Quantum Mechanics
Atheism Sexual Health **Ancient History**
Entrepreneurship Languages Sport
Paleontology Needlework Islam
Metaphysics Investment Archaeology
Parenting Statistics Criminology
Motivational

second-class matter, June 28, 1907, at Brunswick, Maine,

REPORT OF THE PRESIDENT
OF **BOWDOIN COLLEGE**
FOR THE ACADEMIC YEAR, 1927-1928

TOGETHER WITH THE REPORTS OF THE DEAN, THE LIBRARIAN, AND THE DIRECTOR OF THE MUSEUM OF FINE ARTS : : : : : : : : : : :

1927

1928

BRUNSWICK,   MAINE

PRINTED FOR THE COLLEGE,   -   MCMXXVIII

REPORT OF THE PRESIDENT

To the Trustees and Overseers of Bowdoin College:

I have the honor to submit the following report for the academic year 1927-1928.

I. DE MORTUIS

William John Curtis, LL.D., of the class of 1875, died at his summer home in Camden, October 8, 1927, aged seventy-three years. He had been a Trustee of the College since 1915, having previously served as an Overseer since 1901. From 1923 until his death he was chairman of the Finance Committee and was largely responsible for the reorganization of the business methods of the College. The New York *Sun* in an editorial note had the following comment:

> "Mr. Curtis's career includes no passage better illustrative of his fine intellectual and moral qualities than that which records his service on the finance committee at Bowdoin, as a member of which he worked out plans for administration of its property which other endowed institutions of learning have been glad to adapt to meet their own needs. This is an accomplishment better understood by educational executives than it is popularly, but its benefits are bestowed eventually on the public."

Mr. Curtis was such an ideal trustee and he was so well known and beloved in all the circles of the alumni that the College last winter published in one of its bulletins the official tributes paid to his memory; but mere words give after all but little idea of the service he rendered to Bowdoin by his time, his gifts, and above all by his very wonderful character.

The Rev. Edgar Millard Cousins, D.D., of the class of 1877, died at his home in Brewer, Maine, on May 19, 1928, aged seventy-seven years. Dr. Cousins had been an Overseer of the College since 1890 and had given thirty-eight years of patient, self-effacing service to the College in that important position. In 1920 he was honored with the degree of Doctor of Divinity conferred upon him for his devotion as a pastor. He was a modest, kindly, friendly man, and although much handicapped by frail health the last few years was always deeply interested in the affairs of his *Alma Mater.*

II. GIFTS FROM APRIL 1, 1927, TO MARCH 31, 1928

Fellowship in French, Frederick W. Pickard ......$	1,200	00
Delta Upsilon Lecture, Delta Upsilon Fraternity ...	100	00
Lectures, Student Council	135	00
Institute of Art, Society of Bowdoin Women Foundation	200	00
Forbes Rickard, Jr., Prize, Mrs. Forbes Rickard	10	00
Hawthorne Prize, Nora Archibald Smith	80	00
Poetry Prize Fund, anonymous donor (addition) ...	160	00
Poetry Prize (Current Award)	10	00
Library equipment, etc., anonymous donors	7,864	17
Library Serials, John F. Dana	30	00
Books, James E. Rhodes, 2nd	50	00
Lewis Pierce Book Fund (addition), Henry H. Pierce	5,000	00
Canon Fellowes Lectures, Walter V. Wentworth ...	450	00
Land for Athletic Field:		
Frederick W. Pickard	2,000	00
Luther Dana	250	00
John F. Dana	100	00
Fred R. Lord	25	00
George F. Goodspeed	1,000	00
John H. Halford	50	00
William D. Ireland	25	00
Harry Oakes	1,000	00
William M. Ingraham	100	00
Frank H. Swan	350	00
Thomas L. Pierce	50	00
Alfred M. Merriman	25	00
Ralph R. Melloon	5	00
Philip Dana	250	00
Marcus A. Sutcliffe	5	00
William W. Thomas	100	00
Henry H. Pierce	1,000	00
Willard S. Bass	100	00
E. Farrington Abbott	150	00
Henry Lewis	50	00
Alumni Income Fund, contributions by Alumni	5,748	38
President's Loan Fund, Bowdoin Student Loan Association	46	00

Alexander Professorship, Anna Bliss Alexander ... 50,000 00
Davenport Loan Fund, Estate of George P. Daven-
port 5,000 00
Packard Scholarship (addition), anonymous donor 100 00
Swimming Pool Building and Maintenance Funds,
Cyrus H. K. Curtis 200,000 00
Society of Bowdoin Women Foundation (addition) 250 00
Coe Bequest, Estate of Thomas Upham Coe 150,000 00
Pingree Fund, David Pingree 50,000 00
Munsey Bequest, Estate of Frank A. Munsey 250,000 00
Consolidated Scholarship Funds, W. A. Robinson .. 15 00
Coombs Trust Fund, Viola Coombs 7,500 00
Beverly Scholarship Fund (addition), Beverly Men's
Singing Club 115 00
Alexander Scholarship Fund (addition), Estate of
D. S. Alexander 7,238 64
Union Building Fund, Augustus F. Moulton 150,520 54
Alumni Fund, contributions of Alumni 5,837 50
Chapel Organ, Cyrus H. K. Curtis 24,269 40

Total $928,564 63

There are many interesting things in this list of benefactions
to the College. In the first place, the total amount is by far the
largest that the College has ever received in any single year.
In the second place, an analysis of the figures shows that although very generous sums have been given for equipment and
buildings, the endowment for general purposes has been increased by about half a million. If we were adding only material
improvement to our plant, we should of course be fortunate;
but to have, in addition to the buildings we have so long needed,
facilities for improving and strengthening the Faculty should
mean some real progress.

The new chapel organ was dedicated last Commencement and
has been in use throughout the year. It is a very beautiful in-
strument and adds greatly to the dignity of the chapel services;
furthermore, we have had several recitals during the winter
which have been largely attended by students and members of
the community.

The swimming pool given and maintained by Mr. Cyrus H. K. Curtis through his gift of $300,000, was opened for use in January, and as is stated elsewhere in my report, has been used even more than we anticipated.

The very generous gift of a new Union by Augustus F. Moulton, Esq., of the class of '73' announced last Commencement takes again from our list of needs a project that we have carried there for ten years. In April Mr. Moulton gave another $50,000 to the College, making his total gifts for the Union and its furnishings a little over $200,000. The building is now in process of erection and will be open for the use of students early in the year 1929. The cornerstone was laid with appropriate ceremonies on February 27, 1928.

One of the pleasantest gifts we received during the year was that of $50,000 from Mr. David Pingree, of Salem, for the general funds of the College. This gift was unsolicited and came from him on account of his interest in the State of Maine and in the work that Bowdoin is doing.

Since April 1st the College has received a gift of $100,000 from Mr. F. G. Tallman, of Wilmington, Delaware, to establish the Tallman Fund in memory of Bowdoin members of his family, the income to be used to bring to the College from time to time visiting lecturers and professors preferably from abroad. This gift will enable us to carry out some of the recommendations of the committee of the alumni for strengthening the Faculty by distinguished scientists and scholars from abroad and if properly administered should be of very great benefit both to the Faculty and to the students. This benefaction from Mr. Tallman, who is a graduate of Cornell, is a fine example of filial piety, as his father, grandfather, and great-grandfather were graduates or officers of Bowdoin.

In April the College also received a gift of $20,000 from Mrs. William J. Curtis and her children to establish in memory of her husband, William J. Curtis, of the class of '75' a prize to be known as the Bowdoin Prize. This prize which will consist of a large part of the accumulated income of the fund for five years will be awarded once in five years to that graduate, or former member, or member of the Faculty of the College who in the judgment of a committee of award consisting of the Presidents of Harvard and Yale Universities and the Chief

Justice of the Supreme Judicial Court of Maine, has during the period rendered the most distinguished service in any field of human endeavor. The first award of this prize will be made at Commencement in 1933. Such a prize Mr. Curtis himself had in mind to establish believing that it would be intellectually stimulating to both alumni and Faculty; and with characteristic generosity Mrs. Curtis and her children have carried out the project. Mrs. Curtis has also provided funds for a visiting lecturer in Chemistry during one semester of the academic year 1928-29 in accordance with a promise made by Mr. Curtis the day before his death. "He rests from his labors but his works do follow him."

The alumni and friends of the College will be interested to see the gifts for the development of the new athletic field, and will be glad to hear that Mr. Pickard is continuing to support that project, and that the baseball games are now being played in the new field; two tennis courts have been built and are now in use, and football and soccer fields are being fast made ready. It is planned to use the field as a playing field. Whittier Field will be reserved for track and football. The new field will be used for baseball, tennis, Freshman football, soccer, and intra-mural sports of all kinds.

The Class of 1903 is erecting a beautiful gateway to Whittier Field which will be dedicated at Commencement.

To all our generous friends and benefactors both among our alumni and from without, the College is deeply grateful for such evidence of confidence as these notable gifts display, and is fully aware that a deep burden of responsibility is laid on the College for their proper use.

III. CHANGES IN THE FACULTY

During the first semester Professor Gross of the Department of Biology was absent on sabbatical leave doing research work, particularly in ornithology, in Central and South America, spending much of his time in Equador. Professor Dewing of the Department of Greek was also away this semester starting the work at Athens College in Greece of which he is president. Professor Andrews of the Department of Art was on leave the first semester spending much of his time in the museums of

Europe and Egypt. In the second semester the Dean has leave
of absence and made an extended European tour returning to
Brunswick early in May to work on his translation of Plautus
for the Loeb Classical Library. Professor Brown of the Department of Romance Languages is also on leave working in the
Harvard Library. Mr. Austin H. MacCormick, Alumni Secretary, has been away all the year inspecting prisons and otherwise showing that he is fast becoming the successor in prison
reform of the late Thomas Mott Osborne.

Last Commencement Philip Weston Meserve, A.M., was pro-
moted from Assistant Professor to Associate Professor of
Chemistry; Morgan Bicknell Cushing, A.M., from Assistant
Professor to Associate Professor of Economics; Charles Harold
Gray, A.M., from Assistant Professor to Associate Professor of
English; Detlev Walther Schumann, Ph.D., from Instructor to
Assistant Professor of German; Malcolm Elmer Morrell, B.S.,
from Instructor to Assistant Professor of Physical Training,
and Acting Director of Athletics. New appointments were made
as follows: Dr. Henry Lincoln Johnson, College Physician;
Stanley Barney Smith, Ph.D., Associate Professor of the
Classics; Boyd Wheeler Bartlett, A.M., Assistant Professor of
Physics; Walter McKinley Miller, Ph.D., Assistant Professor of
Mathematics; Kenneth James Boyer, A.B., B.L.S., Assistant
Librarian; Robert Channon Pollock, A.M., Instructor in Philosophy and Psychology; Frederick Wilcox Dupee, Ph.B., Instruc-
tor in English; Philip Sawyer Wilder, B.S., Acting Alumni
Secretary; Marcel Charles Camille Bordet, Lic. en Droit, Teach-
ing Fellow in French.

IV. PROGRESS ON THE TEN-YEAR PLAN

In 1925 committees of the undergraduates, of the alumni, and
of the Faculty were appointed to consider the needs of the College during the next ten years, and those committees reported
in the spring of 1926. Our Acting Alumni Secretary, Philip S.
Wilder, has made a careful summary of the recommendations
of these three committees and of the action that has been taken
in the last two years. The committees made the following recommendations for the expansion of our material equipment:
A Union; a new and more extensive playing field; a new chapel
organ; a swimming pool adequately endowed; a new periodical

room in the basement of the Library; the completion of the fifth floor of the stack in the Library; the purchase of a new grand piano for Memorial Hall and an orthophonic victrola for the Department of Music; a gas plant for the Science Department; a gateway to Whittier athletic field. It is gratifying to be able to report that all these needs have been met.

Among other recommendations of the committees were the establishment of a maximum salary of $6,000 for certain professors; the addition of more instructors to the Faculty so that the ratio of instructors to students should be one to ten; the continuation of the Bowdoin Institutes; instruction in modern language departments by a native German and a native Frenchman; the addition of an Assistant Librarian; a skilled mechanician for the Physics Department. It is a pleasure to report that all of these recommendations have been carried out except that, following our policy of adding gradually to the Faculty, we have not yet quite reached the ratio of one instructor to every ten students. We have, however, added an instructor in Economics, in Philosophy and Psychology, in History and Government, in Physical Training, and two men each in the Romance Languages and in English.

Among other recommendations of the committees carried out are the provision for bringing to the College visiting professors or lecturers; the establishment of an alumni quarterly; the continuation of the athletic policy of athletics for all; a better system for reserved books in the Library; and a new method of awarding scholarships.

Studying carefully this summary of recommendations and action taken, it seems to me that, roughly speaking, about eighty per cent. of the suggestions have been carried to fruition in two years. This shows the wisdom of making plans for the future definitely and of submitting those plans to our alumni and friends.

Among the major recommendations not yet carried out should be placed, a publication fund for Faculty and undergraduate works of unusual excellence; the development of the work of the Alumni Secretary; a review of the art collections and the publication of a suitable catalogue; a fund for the purchase of contemporary works of art; the establishment of more graduate scholarships; the requirement of entrance examinations instead of certificates for all candidates for admission; a covered hockey rink; and more suitable provision for the non-fraternity men, although we hope the new Union will in this respect be of avail.

V. NEEDS OF THE COLLEGE

So many of the needs of the College in the last few years have been met that I submit almost an entirely new list:

1. First, last and always, additions to the endowment fund for general collegiate purposes.

2. Funds for the erection of a new heating plant, $150,000 to $200,000.

3. Funds for the renovation of the interior of Memorial Hall, $30,000.

4. Funds for the erection of a little theatre, $50,000.

5. Funds for concerts and recitals, $20,000 to $50,000.

6. Funds for more graduate scholarships, units of $10,000 to $20,000.

7. A covered hockey rink, $30,000 to $40,000.

8. Endowment of a professorship in Biblical Literature, History of Religion, etc., $100,000.

9. Club house for the Faculty.

10. Book funds for the Library.

Undoubtedly within the next two or three years we shall have to make provision for a new heating plant. The present plant on the campus is now being used very nearly up to capacity. Any additional building would so greatly increase the load as to endanger the whole system. Furthermore, the boilers have nearly reached their limit of usefulness. With the increasing attractiveness of the campus it would be very desirable to have a new heating plant off the campus and to have it so large that it could take in the fraternity houses and possibly some of the Faculty houses as well. I shall recommend to the Boards at their meeting the appointment of a committee to investigate the whole problem of heating and to submit plans that will be adequate for the next thirty or forty years. The problem is made easier by the work we have been doing for the last three or four years in the extension of the tunnels.

The College has not yet been obliged to finance any of its major projects by borrowing, and I trust through the generosity of some of our friends we shall be able to make this very necessary improvement within the next two or three years without departing from our usual practice. It is of course true that no one wants to give a memorial heating plant even to keep his memory warm; but on the other hand nothing is more essential in our climate than a modern thoroughly well equipped, economically run heating building.

VI. RELIGION IN THE COLLEGE

The Committee on Religious Interests of which Professor Burnett is the chairman, has recently recommended that increased opportunity for education in religion be offered the students of Bowdoin College through the curriculum, and that there be obtained the services of a full time instructor in the history of religion and in Biblical Literature. Apparently Bowdoin is one of the very few colleges in the country that offers practically no courses in the curriculum devoted to these subjects. To be sure, there is some study and reading of the Bible in Freshman English; a few lectures on the Bible are given in my course in Literature; and every other year Professor Crook offers a course in sociology to a limited group of students on the Social Evolution of the Hebrew People. Nevertheless, it would be well for the College seriously to consider the enrichment of the curriculum along the lines recommended by our committee. In many colleges there is also clearly to be seen an increasing tendency to employ a College Chaplain. The Student Christian Association also makes a strong plea for the employment of a young graduate as full time secretary. The rather small group of undergraduates interested in Christian work has been carrying on heroically; and their wishes should receive most sympathetic consideration.

It is possible that as an experiment we may be able to use next year the income of the Tallman Fund to bring to the College some distinguished English scholar in these fields.

VII. FACULTY SALARIES

There has been a very substantial increase in the compensation for professors during the last ten years. In 1917-1918 the maximum salary was $2,750; today it is for certain members of the Faculty $6,000. It must, however, be remembered that this advance hardly more than covers the increase in the cost of living and while respectable as compared with other institutions is by no means lavish. As President Angell, of Yale, has pointed out in his annual report for this year, the question of compensation for college teachers is one of the most interesting and important now before our educational institutions. There is no reason why a professor should sacrifice the comfort of his wife or the education of his children simply for the sake of being in the teaching profession. The compensation should be placed at such a figure that a man can live in reasonable comfort, make adequate provision for his old age or sickness, educate his children without having to make too great sacrifices, and travel occasionally. For a bachelor, or for a man with some private income, a position in college today is attractive; but for a married man, we have not yet succeeded in making it free from those daily anxieties that beset a man with a family dependent upon his salary. It is, I think, particularly true that a married instructor, or a married assistant professor, has a very hard time of it, and the maximum salary for a professor is not yet so large as it ought to be. I learned the other day at Andover that that school is paying several of its teachers $8,000 a year with housing privileges, thereby setting a splendid example for our colleges.

The College also ought to consider very carefully the whole question of pensions and retiring allowances. Under our present plan teachers who have been appointed since 1915 are on the contributory basis, the College paying so much a year toward the annuity and the individual instructor paying so much. In case of those members of the staff whose appointment dates prior to 1915 it is presumed that they will receive the out and out retiring allowances from the Carnegie Foundation as their predecessors have; but the Foundation has made several changes in its plans and is contemplating other changes. In my judgment there will be no satisfactory solution of the retirement problem until the College supplements the grants that may come from the Carnegie Foundation from its own funds.

There is of course the other side to the shield; if college teachers are well paid and given a reasonable teaching programme, their work should become more and more effective.

The other day a senior in writing a provisional Commencement part took for his subject, "Does the College exist for the Students or for the Professors?" Some college teachers seem to forget that teaching is their primary task and that their teaching time belongs to the undergraduates. I am happy to say that no such condition exists at Bowdoin; but in making plans for increasing salaries it should not be forgotten that as in other professions and occupations a man must in all respects prove himself to be worthy of his hire.

VIII. NEW REGULATIONS

The College Laws provide that the President shall annually report to the Boards for their approval all regulations adopted by the Faculty since their last annual meeting. In accordance with this provision I add a list of such regulations:

1. That the distribution of money allotted from the blanket tax for the support of athletics be under the charge of the Faculty members of the Athletic Council.

2. That no student should be advanced to senior standing unless his modern language requirements are complete.

3. That one year of history be required for admission; and that Ancient History be recommended for students entering the course leading to the degree of A.B.

4. That the Recording Committee no longer admit students who have not actually presented credits in all required subjects.

That no student shall be admitted with free margin credits unless he shall have presented 9 units in concentrated subjects.

That, after 1931, all candidates for the degree of B.S. must present for admission 3 units in foreign languages.

IX. GENERAL EDUCATIONAL POLICY

As this is the close of the tenth year of the present administration it may not be amiss to state once more some of the general principles which are guiding the College in its theories of education. First, it should be remembered that the College is neither a school nor a university. In the first two years and in its elementary courses it necessarily continues some of the methods of the school. In the last two years, and particularly in preparing for the major examination, it tries to inculcate something of the spirit of the university, that spirit where a student works for the love of knowledge for its own sake, and not for what he can in a practical way get out of it, nor for the marks. It is of course true that only a very small proportion of American college boys in any college have anything like a scholarly attitude toward their work. Nevertheless the college holds out the ideal of such scholarship, which is, I believe, more effective than is commonly believed.

The work of the College would of course be easier were the foundations in the schools laid on more uniform and solid lines; but since college years cover the transition from boyhood to young manhood it is doubtful if the College can ever get away entirely from school methods. There are of course many differences between the way in which courses are taught in college and taught in school; in both cases we need more insistently to emphasize thoroughness, but in freshman year particularly we are simply getting ready for work that is to come. The freshman year must always be a transitional one.

As far as our methods of teaching go, we employ the recitation, the lecture, the conference, the tutorial group, and occasionally the tutorial system individually. We hear a good deal said against the lecture system now, and if it were the only method of instruction all the tirades would be justified, but it has some very obvious advantages. It brings the minds of the students into contact with many other minds. It gives them the opportunity of getting very different points of view. When a lecturer does not simply rehearse old lectures or dish up encyclopaedia articles; when, in other words, he gives a fresh impression of his own individual scholarship, very great benefit accrues to the student. And there is something to be said for the so-called snap course. If the teacher of it is a man of real scholarship and learning, his pupils may be quickened in their intellectual life and stimulated. If a very large amount of arduous labor be demanded of them they might not react so effectively. We ought to remember that in the heart of the words *school* and *scholarship* is the Greek word meaning *leisure*. But lectures, whether given in hard or easy courses, ought certainly to be supplemented by group discussion, and that is the purpose of our conferences; and just as in the lecture system the undergraduate comes in contact with different points of view and with different minds of men older and more experienced than himself, so in the conferences he is pitted against the minds of his own contemporaries. The give and take of the conference is a very important factor in education. The maintenance of the conference system is to be sure expensive, for the ideal group in most courses should not be more than six or eight, and a man can properly take on only a limited number of such conferences a week; but as it is the most expensive so it seems to me clearly to be the most effective manner of teaching. It combines all the good points of the formal and informal teaching. In a conference properly conducted no student can escape his responsibility not only for knowledge of the subject but for contributing in discussion of his views to others.

In my inaugural address I said that the undergraduate of today is all too liable to think of his collegiate education as a conglomeration of units or hours or points, not as a unified intellectual accomplishment. It is a pity that our machinery calls for courses and not for subjects. The general examination is an attempt to correct this fault and each year some progress is made in adapting the new system more adequately to our needs. In a few subjects such as physics, chemistry, and mathematics where the advanced work necessarily carries along with it a review of what has gone before, the general examination may not be the best method of testing a knowledge of the subject; but in all other departments I believe unqualifiedly in its worth.

We should look forward to strengthening our educational policy in the following ways: (1) by requiring the passing of some examinations from every candidate for admission; (2) by improving and extending the conference system; (3) by making more and more use, not only in the subject of concentration, but in other ways, of the general examination.

This means more teachers, for it implies more individual instruction. It means a departure from the old and more stereotyped ways of making the course the unit both for instruction and assessment; but it is I am sure a better device for increasing interest in intellectual things.

But whether we use the course, or the general examination, or any other scheme, we ought constantly to remember that these things after all are only the mechanics of the business of education, and that teaching and learning in college depend on bringing together stimulating and experienced instructors and a well prepared student body, and remembering that back of all we undertake we must have a driving spiritual force.

We are all grateful for the advances made in equipment, in funds, in buildings, these past few years; but that makes it all the more necessary for us to remember, that, when all is said and done, in college "we deal with the spirits of men, not with their fortunes," and that while teaching is enhanced and improved by proper surroundings, its success and fruition depend not on them but on the spirit within.

Respectfully submitted,

KENNETH C. M. SILLS.

May 22, 1928.

APPENDIX A

Report of the College Physician

To the President of Bowdoin College:

The group examination of the Freshman Class of 1931 was carried on two days after the opening of college by Doctors Francis J. Welch, Stanwood E. Fisher, Talcott O. Vanamee, and Edwin W. Gehring.

This included examination of heart, lungs, nose and throat, structural system including posture and general surgery. A routine urine examination was made of each man. The result of this examination showed no organic heart conditions; there were two cases of chronic diabetes, five transient albuminurias, besides the usual large proportion of faulty posture.

The body building exercises were carried on by Mr. Cobb and on examination of this class at the end of their course, many showed improvement.

The student body has been encouraged to report promptly all slight illnesses and injuries, and a clinic has been held each morning except Sunday from 8.30 until noon and students have made to date 2917 calls for almost every ailment known to mankind except Beri Beri and Bubonic Plague. This contact has made it possible to help many students particularly those in the Freshman Class to adjust themselves to their new environment and relieve them of different forms of mental anxiety and trouble.

We have been very fortunate this year in not having any contagious or infectious diseases to contend with, and it is comforting to think that this may be due in part to the preventive measures carried out; namely, treating no cases running any temperature, which usually means contagion or infection, in the "ends" or fraternity houses where a friendly call and brotherly care might mean many other cases.

Nose and throat infections have been treated routinely by local measures, entirely preventive, with the result that, with one exception, there has not been a bronchial or lung involvement in the College this year.

Up to this writing sixty-two cases have been cared for in the Infirmary. Three cases, one an incipient pulmonary tuberculosis, one a fractured skull, and one a hemorrhage from an ulcer of the stomach, have been in the Infirmary three weeks or more, otherwise the average stay in the Infirmary has been less than three days.

Eight cases of appendicitis have been operated on and two for repair of hernia.

A series of forty cases of acne have been treated with inoculation and 60% have shown marked improvement.

The X-ray equipment has certainly justified the expenditure, as sixty patients have been X-rayed averaging two pictures per patient. Some of the positive plates have shown incipient tuberculosis, a fractured skull, two broken legs, a broken arm, five fractures of the hand and one rib fracture, besides several infected teeth. If this work had been paid for outside the college the cost would have been much more than the interest on our investment in the X-ray equipment.

There has been a good deal of lost time on the part of the students from infection due to unhygienic conditions of the locker rooms in the gymnasium and I recommend that some decided arrangement be made at the beginning of next semester to take care of this menace.

At this time I wish to thank Mr. Houser for his coöperation in treating many cases with diathermy, under my direction, with the machine given to the Athletic Association by some of the Alumni and would recommend that the Infirmary be supplied with a new machine to relieve in part Mr. Houser in that work.

Respectfully submitted,

HENRY L. JOHNSON, *College Physician.*

APPENDIX B

Report on the Swimming Pool

To the President of Bowdoin College:

The following facts concerning the sanitation of the Bowdoin Swimming Pool are submitted for your information.

Once or twice a day a quantity of sodium hypochlorite solution has been added to the pool for the purpose of destroying bacteria. The amount of this solution used to dose the pool is determined by a test of the amount of available chlorine in the water and also by the pool load, i.e., the number of swimmers using the pool during a given period of time. Thus it has been necessary for a record of the pool attendance to be kept in the pool laboratory. The following figures are of interest.

The total attendance from January 3 to March 30 (the winter term) was 6355 or an average of about 77 per day.

The total attendance from March 30 to May 10 was 1370 or an average of about 35 per day. Classes in swimming have not been held since the termination of the winter term.

The total attendance from January 3 to May 10 was 7725.

I believe that the majority of the students have coöperated intelligently in keeping the pool clean. The available chlorine in the water has been maintained betwen 0.1 and 0.5 part per million. The bacteria count has been gratifyingly low except at those times when swimming meets have been held and persons have walked in shoes on the pool deck. There is no doubt moreover that the use of swimming suits increases the bacteria count. But, at no time has the water given a positive presumptive test for the B. coli group, which indicates a very desirable freedom from sewage contamination.

We are particularly fortunate in having no algae problem with which to deal. At no time since the water was first put into the pool has there appeared the slightest indication of a growth of algae.

Respectfully submitted,

PHILIP W. MESERVE.

APPENDIX C

Religious Preference 1927-1928

Congregational	187
Episcopal	86
Baptist	51
Methodist	48
Unitarian	44
Roman Catholic	35
Universalist	30
Presbyterian	25
Jewish	13
Lutheran	6
Christian Science	5
Friends	3
Dutch Reformed	2
Swedenborgian	2
Greek Orthodox	1
Reformed Church of America	1
Christian	1
No preference	9
	549

REPORT OF THE ACTING DEAN

To the President of Bowdoin College:

Sir:—It is only in obedience to custom that I address my report to you; for I am aware that you keep so closely in touch with all the inner workings of the College that any information which I shall give will be to you but a twice-told tale. In reality, then, it is the Governing Boards and the Alumni and other interested friends of the College that I have in mind as I write these words.

When I took up the work at the beginning of the semester, I found that Dean Nixon had left behind him no unseemly clutter, but, in keeping with his accustomed efficiency, he had set his house in order and about to go into a far country "had carefully delivered unto his servants his goods." And I have hoped, since he is not an austere man reaping where he has not sown and gathering where he has not strewn, that upon his return he may not desire to cast any of us into outer darkness. Indeed I have cherished the hope of passing the Office over to him in as good condition as it was when I took it — with no knotty problems unsolved, with no official prestige lost, and, at all odds, with no troublesome precedents established.

"The Dean's job is the most disagreeable one connected with any college," the father of three fine Bowdoin graduates said to me not long ago. And perhaps it may seem thus at times. Possibly in some troubled moment one may feel like paraphrasing King Henry's words and exclaiming:

> "Upon the Dean! let us our lives, our souls,
> Our debts . . . . . .
> Our children and our sins lay on the Dean.
> He must bear all."

And yet, Mr. President, as you who were Dean for eight years and more well know, there is much in his work that helps to keep his life from seeming "stale, flat, and unprofitable." His task certainly is more than the fingering of card catalogues, more than the listening to "rationalized" excuses for class or chapel cuts, more than the dictating of letters to fond parents and solicitous principals explaining why their sons have failed to live up to their inheritance or their former students to follow in the ways of their wise instruction. .The more one knows of the Dean's work the more he may suspect that, like that of teaching, the Dean's is "a petty business for the petty-minded but a noble profession for the noble-hearted." In the Dean's office, possibly more than anywhere else, a man has a chance to see the student at his worst and also at his best, to analyze his failings, to discover whether his flesh is strong or weak, his spirit brave or cowardly, to know many of his perplexities, to become acquainted with his financial worries and his home difficulties, to share his regrets for past follies, his doubts concerning his ability to wrestle with the world or his brave hopes for future success.

It is an opportunity which any interested observer of modern life may well envy — this of examining close up and at first hand that much misunderstood species of the *genus homo,* the American college student. For, much as he has been discussed during the last century, was there ever a time when the people as a whole were more interested in him or more critical of him than they are today? He is scrutinized and analyzed and characterized from many points of view. He is front-page material for the Sunday Supplement and rare is the magazine writer who does not essay to take a fall out of him. A semester's work as Acting Dean, however, has not caused me to modify in any important way the opinion which thirty years or more of college teaching have led me to have of him. Now and then there is, of course, a man in college who is obviously out of his element, who is too lazy and doesn't care, who hasn't the intellect to comprehend the significance of what he is studying or the emotional and spiritual equipment to keep him from "sniggering" at those ideals of human conduct or those standards of artistic expression which centuries have proved good. But such an exception is rare. Certainly the average college student is far from being the brutal, moronic, bawdy-minded sensualist, caring nothing for the finer things of life, which sensational writers would have the uninitiated think he is. If he is not always a Sir Galahad, one thing is certain; he is seldom an Elmer Gantry. Silly, impetuous, indolent, selfish, conceited, not grown-up, — all these he may sometimes be; but for the most part he is a healthy-minded, thoughtful, ambitious, eager-hearted lad, not over-scholarly, but clean and sane and sound.

In keeping the student body worthy of Bowdoin's best traditions, the methods and requirements of admission play an important part. This question of entrance requirements is far from being a new one. It does, however, call for constant and careful consideration, especially at present, when the demand for a college education is still on the increase and educational ideals and scholastic curricula and methods are rapidly changing. The springing up of Junior Colleges on the one hand and particularly of Junior High Schools on the other may well lead any college to evaluate again its entrance requirements and its methods of admission. That, as you know, Mr. President, a committee of our Faculty has done during the past year; and I believe that its conclusions are sound: Generally that college preparation is best which enables the candidate to offer for entrance credit "fairly large bills instead of small change." Experience seems to show that in preparatory work considerable concentration is highly desirable and that four studies pursued for four years each give better college preparation than sixteen for one year each. It is probably not a mere happening that in the present Freshman Class, according to the Abraxas Cup rating, the men with high concentration in their preparatory work showed an average score of 9.25 while the men with practically no concentration showed a score of only 5.3, or that the eight men in the class who secured the best grades for their first semester all presented high concentration in entrance credits. These and many similar facts seem to show, along with other things, that the new Junior High School, if it wishes to give its students who are going to college their best preparation, should make provision for the study of Algebra and Latin, as well as English and History, and possibly French, during its last year. To allow a boy in the Junior High or the Senior High to nibble at this or sip at that in order to test his taste may possibly be useful in helping him to make a choice but it is liable to injure his preparation for the liberal college.

Again, although the time is not yet ripe, one may prophesy that in no distant future many colleges of Bowdoin's standard will require their candidates for admission to pass the College Board examinations in at least two of their principal studies,

and probably in all, instead of allowing them to enter, as now,
by certificate. It is worth noting that the larger colleges for
women, when they wished to restrict their numbers and raise
their standards and secure more scholarly students, did something of this very sort.

But to keep Bowdoin students up to the standard involves
more than entrance requirements. It also concerns methods of
teaching. A significant change is today taking place in some
American colleges — a change that may well give us pause. I
refer to the abolition of required attendance at recitations and
lectures and in some cases a doing away with class recitations
altogether and a frank adoption of the so-called Oxford or
tutorial method. This change arises of course from a desire to
avoid the dangers of mass teaching and to reap the advantages
of individual instruction. It probably shows a tendency in the
right direction. Surely American universities have sometimes
suffered much because of their attempts to wholesale rather than
retail education. But one who has been watching educational
methods for some years cannot but advise a college like Bowdoin
to hasten slowly in the adoption of these new methods. As we
read of some of the drastic changes in college methods and requirements, we cannot help having what Dean Briggs characterized some years ago as "old-fashioned doubts about new-
fashioned education." The Oxford method would undoubtedly
be good for some students under favorable conditions — for
perhaps fifty at Bowdoin — but we must not make the mistake
of thinking that it will work well with all students, in all colleges, at all times, and that it is a panacea for all educational
diseases.

In this connection one cannot but recall the high hopes and
exaggerated expectations with which American educators forty
years ago hailed the coming of the elective system. The shackles
which had retarded the progress of learning were at last to be
stricken off. College youths were no longer to be bound hand
and foot by hateful curricular requirements. They were no
longer to be obliged to travel in narrow and prescribed paths
through dark forests and dismal swamps. But now they were
to trip as fancy pleased through sunlit and daisied fields of
learning and perhaps could even mount "like a strong bird
on pinion free." Education henceforth was to be freed from

drudgery and everybody was to be wise and at the same time happy, for all were to seek learning only where natural desire led the way. The method doubtless did do good but the results fell far short of expectations. Before many years it was discovered that boys were electing courses not simply because they loved learning but also because they loved ease. Boys still were boys and the elective system had not suddenly transformed them into zealous, mature, hard-working, truth-seeking scholars. "Pipe" courses became popular; and afternoon courses, no matter in what or by whom, were regarded as hateful interferences and were shunned because they collided with athletic sports. The result was that often a student's college record, his "blue-card," showed a disorganized conglomeration of courses having no special relation to each other and no special bearing upon his future career. And it has been interesting to watch the pendulum swing back; so that today with required Freshman courses, with special requirements in modern languages, with group requirements, with major and minor course requirements, and major examination requirements, the much-vaunted elective system has come to be hardly more than a name.

Such may possibly be the history of the Oxford movement in American colleges. It is doubtless true that "Oxford" is a name to conjure with and that the great English university has been successful in educating many an eminent scholar by the method of allowing him to attend lectures only when he wished or having him meet his tutor — a learned and stimulating teacher — and be "smoked at," as Stephen Leacock puts it, for only one hour a week. But even though that be so, it is not convincing. American college students are not English students. Many of them do not have the intellectual background of the Oxford men. In America we do not wish to restrict our college opportunities simply to those that have that background. Regret it or not we are sending, and are bound to send, more men into the arena of business than into fields of scholarship. The boys that come into our colleges need the give and take of the recitation room and the careful, almost daily, guidance and supervision not of one instructor but of several. The Oxford method has grown up gradually, has been moulded and made effective by the social and educational institutions and customs of a country where there is still much of caste and class and also a long tradition of scholarship and learning. A semester in the Dean's office of almost any American college like Bowdoin should convince a man that to try to transplant such a system bodily from an ancient university in a country like England to an American college in a democracy like ours is to court disappointment if not disaster.

I know, Mr. President, that this is probably contrary to the opinion which for various reasons is popular among undergraduates, but I feel sure that this advice is sound for Bowdoin: We should meet our students in small groups if possible; we should emphasize the power of personality in teaching and the value of individual instruction; we should not be ignorant of what has been called the alchemy of human influence; but in doing away with class attendance, in allowing the student to cut recitations and lectures at pleasure, to go or come according to his own sweet will, — that way, I am convinced, lies danger. It is possible to have too much Oxford.

I. ENROLLMENT

Number of
Students enrolled Sept. 22, 1927 ....555 (Sept. 23, 1926—544)
Students enrolled Dec.   1, 1927 ....548 (Dec.   1, 1926—537)
   Left between Sept. 22nd and Dec. 1st 7
Students enrolled April 1, 1928 522
   Left between Dec. 1st and April 1, 1928 31
   Seniors finishing work for degree 4
   Men re-admitted 5

	Dec. 1, 1927	April 1, 1928
Students in Senior Class	94	89
Students in Junior Class	120	119
Students in Sophomore Class (inc. 1 Special)	157	151
Students in Freshman Class (inc. 3 Specials)	177	163
	548	522

II. GEOGRAPHICAL DISTRIBUTION OF STUDENTS

Maine	251
Massachusetts	192
New York	25
New Jersey	19
New Hampshire	14
Connecticut	13
Pennsylvania	9
Rhode Island	6
Illinois	5
Ohio	4
Maryland	3
Iowa	2
Michigan	2
Virginia	2
California	1
Delaware	1
Indiana	1
Nebraska	1
Texas	1
Mexico	1
Porto Rico	1
Sweden	1
Total	555

III. MAINE RESIDENTS AT BOWDOIN COLLEGE

County	No.
Androscoggin	32
Aroostook	17
Cumberland	82
Franklin	10
Hancock	4
Kennebec	17
Knox	10
Lincoln	3
Oxford	10
Penobscot	24
Piscataquis	4

Sagadahoc		5
Somerset		10
Waldo		2
Washington		9
York		12
		251

IV. ENROLLMENT IN COURSES 1927-1928

Course	First Semester	Second Semester
Art 2a		26
Art 6a		30
Astronomy 1, 2	6	5
Botany		17
Chemistry 1, 2	97	90
Chemistry 3, 4	30	24
Chemistry 5, 6	12	14
Chemistry 7, 8	14	13
Chemistry 9, 10	10	5
Economics 1, 2	91	88
Economics 3, 4	16	16
Economics 6		7
Economics 9, 10	20	19
Economics 11, 12	6	21
English 1, 2	172	166
English 4		175
English 5, 6		26
English 7, 8	14	15
English 9, 10	7	4
English 11, 12	69	61
English 13, 14	79	74
English 17, 18	52	52
English 21, 22	11	9
English 25, 26	33	33
French 3, 4	163	159
French 5, 6	69	67
French 7, 8	18	17
French 9, 10	8	8
French 15, 16	7	6

German 1, 2	97	71
German 3, 4	32	26
German 5, 6	33	26
German 7, 8	17	13
German 9, 10	13	10
German 11, 12	7	7
German 13, 14	2	2
Government 1, 2	132	130
Government 3, 4	34	33
Government 7, 8	21	23
Government 9, 10	37	36
Greek A, B	28	25
Greek 1, 2	19	16
Greek 3, 4	8	5
Greek 11, 12	9	39
Greek 13, 14	2	2
History 3, 4	68	58
History 5, 6	19	16
History 9, 10	32	31
History 11, 12	16	16
History 13, 14	16	20
Latin A, B	14	15
Latin 1, 2	39	40
Latin 5, 4	7	9
Latin 9, 8	7	8
Literature 1, 2	93	89
Mathematics 1, 2	138	142
Mathematics 3, 4	24	22
Mathematics 5, 6	11	10
Mathematics 7, 8	4	4
Mathematics 9, 12	7	2
Mineralogy		17
Music 1, 2	38	33
Music 3, 4	11	7
Music 5, 6	2	
Philosophy 1, 2	78	65
Philosophy 3, 6	38	32
Physics 1, 2	51	45
Physics 3, 4	49	45
Physics 5, 6	5	3

Psychology 1, 2 68   60
Psychology 3, 4 19   12
Psychology 5, 6 8   8
Sociology 1, 2 45
Spanish 1, 2 88   75
Spanish 3, 4 15   11
Surveying 1 3
Zoölogy 1, 2 43   39
Zoölogy 6 11
Zoölogy 9, 12 49   5

V. STUDENT COUNCIL CUP STANDING

February, 1928

Non-Fraternity 10.709
Zeta Psi 10.266
Chi Psi 10.142
Kappa Sigma 9.880
Delta Upsilon 9.439
Phi Delta Psi 9.282
Beta Theta Pi 9.268
Delta Kappa Epsilon 9.137
Sigma Nu 8.976
Theta Delta Chi 8.450
Psi Upsilon 7.871
Alpha Delta Phi 7.846

VI. STUDENT COUNCIL CUP 1911-1928

Date	Fraternity	High Average	General Average
Feb., 1911	Delta Upsilon	11.9683	10.0209
June, 1911	Delta Upsilon	15.3050	12.2834
Feb., 1912	Delta Upsilon	12.1700	10.0515
June, 1912	Delta Upsilon	15.7500	13.1750
Feb., 1913	Delta Upsilon	12.7750	10.4801
June, 1913	Delta Upsilon	15.9700	13.6332
Feb., 1914	Delta Upsilon	11.6150	9.7038
June, 1914	Delta Upsilon	13.6700	12.4385
Feb., 1915	Bowdoin Club	11.3513	9.9176
June, 1915	Bowdoin Club	14.1350	12.8082
Feb., 1916	Beta Chi (now Sigma Nu)	12.1360	10.3430
June, 1916	Alpha Delta Phi	14.9400	12.9990

Feb., 1917	Phi Theta Upsilon (now Chi Psi)	12.6890	10.6470
June, 1917	Phi Theta Upsilon (now Chi Psi)	15.9190	12.4940
Feb., 1918	Phi Theta Upsilon (now Chi Psi)	13.1000	11.1353
June, 1918	Phi Theta Upsilon (now Chi Psi)	17.0830	14.2610
Mar., 1918	Chi Psi	11.7000	10.1637
June, 1919	Not available		
Feb., 1920	Zeta Psi	10.1818	9.2534
June, 1920	Theta Delta Chi	12.6000	11.5920
Feb., 1921	Zeta Psi	13.6666	12.5949
June, 1921	Phi Delta Psi	13.6666	12.5949
Feb., 1922	Phi Delta Psi	10.3673	8.1516
June, 1922	Phi Delta Psi	11.2800	9.0321
Feb., 1923	Chi Psi	9.2179	7.9641
June, 1923	Delta Upsilon	12.1143	10.5400
Feb., 1924	Phi Delta Psi	11.2419	9.1254
June, 1924	Phi Delta Psi	14.0500	11.4241
Feb., 1925	Phi Delta Psi	11.0270	8.9190
June, 1925	Phi Delta Psi	13.7297	11.7922
Feb., 1926	Phi Delta Psi	11.5520	9.4346
June, 1926	Phi Delta Psi	11.1527	9.8634
Feb., 1927	Delta Upsilon	11.3610	9.5709
June, 1927	Beta Theta Pi	10.3680	9.6370
Feb., 1928	Zeta Psi	10.7090	9.2720

This cup has been awarded 34 times, 10 times to Delta Upsilon, 4 times to Phi Theta Upsilon, which is now Chi Psi, 9 times to Phi Delta Psi, the local fraternity, 3 times to Zeta Psi, twice to the Bowdoin Club which no longer exists, twice to Chi Psi, and once each to Alpha Delta Phi, Theta Delta Chi, Beta Chi which is now Sigma Nu, and Beta Theta Pi. The non-fraternity group had the highest average for nine semesters but since the cup is awarded to a fraternity or club, this fact does not appear above.

The general average is the average of the whole college at the time of each award.

The average of the general average, or the average of scholarship since 1911 is 10.4238.

The average of the winners' averages is 12.2616.

VII. ABRAXAS CUP STANDING

February, 1928

	Per cent	Grades
Deering High School (6 men)	15.166	91.0
Bangor High School (3 men)	12.000	36.0
Winthrop (Mass.) High School (4 men)	12.000	48.0

Houlton High School (4 men) 11.000   44.0
Phillips-Exeter Academy (5 men) 10.600   53.0
Hebron Academy (6 men) 10.166   61.0
Brunswick High School (4 men) 10.000   40.0
Portland High School (4 men) 10.000   40.0
Wilbraham Academy (3 men) 10.000   30.0
Edward Little High School (6 men) 9.333   56.0
Morse High School (3 men) 8.333   25.0
Watertown (Mass.) High School (3 men) ... 8.333   25.0
Newton (Mass.) High School (5 men) 7.200   36.0
Huntington School, Boston (4 men) 6.250   25.0
Deerfield Academy (6 men) 4.000   24.0

VIII. ABRAXAS CUP—1915-1928

Date	Winner	Winning Average	Average of all Schools Competing
Feb., 1915	Exeter Academy	15.1250	10.0740
Feb., 1916	Portland H. S.	11.9000	9.1180
Feb., 1917	Dexter H. S.	12.8333	9.6207
Feb., 1918	Skowhegan H. S.	15.8333	10.6560
Feb., 1919	Edward Little H. S.	11.3333	10.0694
Feb., 1920	Jordan H. S.	11.3333	8.6548
Feb., 1921	Brunswick H. S.	15.1250	8.7295
Feb., 1922	Portland H. S.	13.6600	8.4650
Feb., 1923	Deering H. S.	12.6000	6.6676
Feb., 1924	Brunswick H. S.	12.2727	9.0245
Feb., 1925	Bangor H. S.	8.8423	8.0235
Feb., 1926	Livermore Falls H. S.	12.6250	8.5400
Feb., 1927	Deering H. S.	16.0000	10.6100
Feb., 1928	Deering H. S.	15.1666	9.6254

General average—9.1341.

Winning average—13.1892.

The averages are obtained on the basis of, A equalling 4; B, 3; C, 2; D, 1; and E, —2.

Although the real work of the College can never be accurately expressed in figures, the foregoing tables concerning the enrollment of the students and their geographical distribution, as well as the results of scholarship competition, both by fraternities and individuals, may help to give some indication of the kind of students we have had and what they have been doing during the last year.

Respectfully submitted,

WILMOT B. MITCHELL, *Acting Dean.*

REPORT OF THE LIBRARIAN

To the President of Bowdoin College:

In accordance with the laws of the College I present herewith my 13th annual report on the condition and progress of the College Library for the year ending 31 March, 1928, the same being the 28th-29th year of my connection with the Library.

SIZE AND GROWTH

The number of volumes in the Library is estimated to be 141,700. The accessions for the past twelve months were 3,280 volumes; of which number 2,575 were purchased, 2,124 at an average cost of $2.71, and 451 by subscription to periodicals that were bound; and, 703 came by gift, — 178 from the State and National governments by provision of law, and 525 from various persons and institutions. As heretofore, the Appendix to this report gives an itemized statement of the growth of the collection during the year and its contents by the various classes in which it is arranged.

PURCHASES

Expenditures for books during the past year approached very closely the high mark of two years ago, and when the other items, viz., periodicals and binding, that go to make up the increase of the library are taken into consideration, a new high mark has been set. This should be expected, and should increase from year to year for some time at least.

The purchases have been spread among the various departments of instruction where they were most needed, and it is difficult to pick out the most important additions.

It is always a matter of satisfaction to record the completion of any extensive work, and this year has seen our set of the Berichte der Deutschen Chemischen Gesellschaft made perfect, and the Oxford New English Dictionary brought to a close.

The excess income of the Smyth Mathematical Prize Fund, which, unknown to anyone, should have been turned over to the Library annually for the purchase of books had been allowed to accumulate until it had reached the sum of $567.45. Last year this sum was transferred to the Library for the purchase of mathematical works. Negotiations have been under way for several months and two important sets have been added, which, under normal conditions we never could have hoped to secure. These are the volumes so far published of Courant's Grundlehren der Mathematischen Wissenschaften, and the Encyklopädie der Mathematischen Wissenschaften. One or two other important sets will be added from the above income during the coming year.

While considering the subject of purchases it is interesting to keep in mind that about 80% of our accessions are selected and purchased after due thought. Gifts are not belittled in this statement, as the Library comes by many valuable things through gift that it could never secure in any other way, but when the proportion of gifts to total accessions approaches one-half it is a condition to be deplored unless the gifts are of a most unusual character. Our very high proportion of 80% purchases should be maintained not by discouraging gifts but by keeping appropriations up to a point that will leave gifts under 25% of our accessions.

In this connection it should be stated that we cannot properly catalogue and care for more new books than we are now able to buy. If a larger number of books are to be cared for annually an increase in the cataloguing force will be necessary. However, there is one very important line along which many thousands of dollars can and should be spent without the necessity of an increased staff. This is completing periodical sets, and adding a few new titles. The Library is very well off in periodical literature, but there are a great many incomplete sets, and references are constantly being made to the volumes that we never had. Twenty-five years ago we could add a new periodical to our list but we could not afford to buy the back volumes. During the last quarter of a century a large number of university and public libraries, especially in the west, have been buying up periodical sets, with the result that it costs twice as much now to complete a set as it did then. The end is not yet, and competition is growing keener, so that if we do not complete our sets within the next decade many of them will never be completed. Speaking within the terms that limit our thoughts, an almost indefinite amount could be spent on periodical sets without increasing our expenses for administration.

GIFTS

While no new fund has been added to the library endowment, considerable additions have been made to some funds through gifts and profit on securities. Henry Hill Pierce, of the Class of 1896, made a further contribution of $5,000 to the fund which he established last year in memory of his father, Lewis Pierce, of the Class of 1852, and through the sale of securities previously given by Mr. Pierce the principle sum of the fund has approached $19,000 making it the second largest fund devoted to the uses of the Library.

Checks have also been received from James E. Rhodes, of the Class of 1897; John F. Dana, of the Class of 1898; and Mrs. William J. Curtis.

CIRCULATION

The number of books charged to borrowers for use outside the library building during the past year was 8,264. The largest number of loans in a single month was 1,221, in March; the smallest 278, in June.

The total circulation is more than a thousand greater than that of the previous year, and the largest since 1912. Why it was exceeded in 1912, and also in 1910, 1902, 1898, and 1897, no guess is ventured and no reason can be given. The number of loans in March is the largest number recorded since circulation figures have been kept.

Of course circulation can be increased or decreased, within certain limitations, more or less at will, and the increase of last year is pretty definitely attributable to the purchase of more recent books. A shelf of new books, composed mostly of fiction, but also containing biography, travel, poetry, drama, and occasionally other even more solid material, has been kept near the charging desk in the most prominent place in the Library. The circulation of these books has been limited to seven days each and a rapid turnover has been insured. The record kept of the circulation of books from this shelf accounts for a large part of the increase in the circulation of the year. But then, this is a way of promoting the habit of reading, and that is one of the chief functions of a library.

THE NEW READING ROOM

The students' reading room has been continued under the same general plan as last year. The newness has worn off and it may be fairly considered to be beyond the stage of an experiment. The attendance has fallen off somewhat* if counted in students per day, but if counted in hours of reading it has probably increased, because, while last year many students came to the room for a few minutes at a time and looked around and took down several books without reading any, this year their visits have lengthened into an hour or two and in most cases each visit has been devoted to a single volume. Desultory reading and browsing have given way to the reading of whole books, and when the character of the collection is taken into consideration it would seem that a desirable and natural change had come about.

UNION LIST OF SERIALS

For the past four years a good deal of time has been put in as one of the coöperating libraries in the preparation of the *Union List of Serials in Libraries of the United States and Canada*. While we cannot claim to have made large contributions to this great bibliographical undertaking, we were the only coöperating library in Maine, and we have performed a duty imposed upon us in accepting the distinct honor of being asked to be one of the coöperators. This work has come to an end and the resulting volume has already proved its worth.

LIBRARY OF CONGRESS CATALOGUE

The Library has been a depository of the printed catalogue cards of the Library of Congress since near the beginning of the undertaking. There are only 57 depository libraries, 48 being in the United States, and Bowdoin being the only one in the State of Maine. This catalogue forms the greatest bibliographical service in the United States and it is constantly increasing in usefulness. Again we have come to a critical period in housing the cards and it seems inevitable that new cases costing nearly a thousand dollars will have to be provided next year.

---

* The attendance has been about twice as great as in a similar room in a similar college.

FINANCIAL STATEMENT

The following table presents a classified statement of the sources of the income and the nature of the expenditures of the Library, arranged substantially along the lines recommended by the American Library Association.

RECEIPTS

	1924-25	1925-26	1926-27	1927-28
Appropriations, salaries ..	$5,225 00	$5,825 00	$6,000 00	$8,400 00
Books, etc.	4,737 50	5,150 00	5,150 00	5,150 00
Endowment funds, consol.	2,030 92	2,134 86	2,094 67	2,043 89
Appleton fund	650 48	713 87	544 00	530 82
Chapman memorial ...	169 83	240 64	336 90	328 76
Class of 1899 fund			22 54	87 08
Class of 1875 fund	120 00	104 98	90 87	88 71
Drummond fund	211 80	225 07	168 01	163 99
Hubbard fund	4,601 31	4,221 12	4,629 07	4,713 73
Thomas Hubbard fund	187 91	175 59	178 94	174 61
Lynde fund	69 08	56 92	80 41	78 48
Morse fund ....:...			45 24	52 68
W. A. Packard fund ..	250 52	318 86	270 57	264 03
Pierce fund			88 92	699 58
Smyth fund				567 45
Stanwood fund		16 90	68 73	67 06
Gifts, etc.	2,268 84	112 70	1,265 50	6,364 18
	$20,523 19	$19,296 51	$21,034 37	$29,775 05

EXPENDITURES

	1924-25	1925-26	1926-27	1927-28
Books	$3,751 53	$6,182 21	$5,408 83	$5,983 62
Periodicals	1,053 08	1,278 32	1,349 57	1,388 93
Binding	733 43	939 86	994 11	1,258 58
Express and postage	103 31	195 34	166 37	233 64
Increase of Library ..	[5,641 35]	[8,595 73]	[7,918 88]	[8,864 77]
Library supplies	256 29	405 70	401 39	512 54
Salaries, library service ..	7,846 15	8,923 21	9,076 09	11,658 66
janitor service ..	932 13	930 96	1,070 97	1,294 67
New equipment	2,488 18	53 90	734 10	7,873 43
Repairs	407 08	532 28	512 56	451 87
Supplies for building	35 10	33 03	109 80	73 93
Telephone	34 75	41 65	48 80	53 50
	$17,641 03	$19,516 46	$19,872 59	$30,783 37

ENDOWMENT FUNDS

I add a table of the Endowment Funds of the Library in order that the preceding table may be more intelligible and that the various funds and their donors may be recorded.

Name of Fund	Established by	1927	1928
John Appleton	Fred'k H. Appleton	$9,997 50	$10,052 50
Chapman Memorial	Frederic H. Gerrish	6,103 50	6,103 50
Class of 1899	Class of 1899	1,648 52	1,648 52
Class of 1875	Class of 1875	1,500 00	1,500 00
Samuel H. Ayer	Athenæan Society	1,000 00	1,000 00
Bond	Elias Bond	7,082 00	7,082 00
Bowdoin	George S. Bowdoin	1,020 00	1,020 00
Philip H. Brown	John C. Brown	2,000 00	2,000 00
Class of 1877	Class of 1877	1,013 34	1,013 34
Class of 1882	Class of 1882	2,300 54	2,300 54
Class of 1890	Class of 1890	1,000 00	1,000 00
Class of 1901	Class of 1901	713 34	713 34
Cutler	John L. Cutler	1,000 00	1,000 00
Fiske	John Orr Fiske	1,000 00	1,000 00
General Fund	Several persons	1,364 28	2,770 78
Hakluyt	Robert Waterston	1,100 00	1,100 00
Alpheus S. Packard	Sale of publications	500 00	500 00
Patten	John Patten	500 00	500 00
Sherman	Mrs. John C. Dodge	2,176 92	2,176 92
Sibley	Jonathan L. Sibley	6,958 37	6,958 37
Walker	Joseph Walker	5,248 00	5,248 00
Wood	Robert W. Wood	1,000 00	1,000 00
	Consolidated	$36,976 79	$38,383 29
James Drummond	Mrs. Drummond and daughter	3,045 00	3,045 00
Hubbard	Thomas H. Hubbard	79,629 07	85,875 37
Thomas Hubbard	His sisters and brother	3,066 96	3,066 96
Frank J. Lynde	George S. Lynde	1,486 24	1,486 24
Morse	Edward S. Morse	1,000 00	1,000 00
W. A. Packard	William A. Packard	5,000 00	5,000 00
Lewis Pierce	Henry Hill Pierce	6,500 00	18,807 00
Stanwood	Edward Stanwood	1,269 72	1,269 72
		$157,223 30	$177,238 10

NEW CONSTRUCTION

The lower periodical room has been equipped with tables, chairs, and lights and has been in use during the entire year. This room has enabled us to smooth out most of the awkward situations arising in the use of periodicals.

The eastern half of the fifth floor of the stack has been equipped with steel bookcases and the 200's (Religion) have been moved there from the first floor. The entire first floor has been rearranged to occupy the space thus made vacant and the whole stack is now for the first time in many years in good condition.

The heating pipes and electric wires have not been extended to the fifth floor of the stack and it is doubtful if it will be necessary to extend the heat beyond its present level. The absence of lights, however, restricts the use of the fifth floor considerably in the winter time, and provision should be made before long for constructing the fifth glass floor and lighting the newly completed fifth floor. The fifth glass floor will carry the sixth floor of the stack thus completing the original plan. It will not be necessary to erect the sixth floor for a few years.

A new counter has been installed in the southwestern corner of the main reading room, enclosing a space about 10 feet square. This construction was made necessary by the increased use of books reserved by the instructors for required reading in the various courses offered in the College. We have, therefore, followed the long procession of libraries that have been compelled to resort to the method of "closed" or restricted shelves for a large part of the reserved books. The adaptability of the building has made it possible to render this new service without in any way hurting the appearance of the main reading room.

ADMINISTRATION

From the opening of Hubbard Hall in 1903, it was recognized that efficient service could not be rendered with fewer than three men. From the death of Dr. Little in 1915 the staff remained short-handed till a year ago when a new Assistant Librarian was elected. Mr. Kenneth J. Boyer was graduated from the University of Rochester in 1923 and from the New York State Library School in 1925. For the next two years he was Librarian of the Westfield (Mass.) Atheneum. His coming to the Library has enabled us to remedy many shortcomings that we were sorely conscious of, and to render service such as we have been unable to give the users of the Library for several years.

Mr. Lewis's services of nearly twenty years were recognized by the title of Reference Librarian.

Respectfully submitted,

GERALD G. WILDER, *Librarian.*

Hubbard Hall, 30 April, 1928.

APPENDIX

The Library, as Classified, showing Accessions for the Period From April 1, 1927, to March 31, 1928.

Divisions	Subject Number	Bought	Given	Added	Total
Bibliography	010	29	8	37	1,336
Library economy	020	4	3	7	702
General encyclopædias	030	2		2	981
General collected essays	040				44
General periodicals	050	94	3	97	7,330
General societies	060	1	1	2	208
Newspapers	070	63		63	1,486
Special libraries	080				386
Book rarities	090		3	3	77
Philosophy	100	15		15	373
Metaphysics	110	1		1	50
Special metaphysical topics	120				54
Mind and body	130	17		17	386
Philosophical systems	140				32
Psychology	150	20		20	514
Logic	160	1		1	92
Ethics	170	12	4	16	898
Ancient philosophers	180	6		6	103
Modern philosophers	190	26		26	659
Religion	200	20	3	23	1,880
Natural theology	210	1		1	322
Bible	220	5	1	6	1,872
Doctrinal theology	230				997
Practical and devotional	240	1			429
Homiletical, pastoral, parochial	250		1	1	879
Church, institutions, work	260	6	1	7	926
Religious history	270	14		14	904
Christian churches, sects	280	5	2	7	1,192
Non-Christian religions	290	8		8	358

Sociology	300	47	1	48	1,136
Statistics	310	9	2	11	810
Political science	320	93	20	113	4,207
Political economy	330	109	38	147	4,186
Law	340	52	51	103	3,346
Administration	350	28	7	35	2,893
Associations, institutions	360	14	12	26	1,116
Education	370	24	26	50	4,035
Commerce, communication	380	13	54	67	1,948
Customs, costumes, folk lore	390	8	3	11	262
Philology	400	17		17	560
Comparative	410				94
English	420	4	1	5	438
German	430	3		3	382
French	440	13	1	14	377
Italian	450	1		1	49
Spanish	460				56
Latin	470				334
Greek	480				287
Minor languages	490				164
Natural science	500	55	23	78	2,696
Mathematics	510	10	2	12	1,257
Astronomy	520	12	9	21	1,304
Physics	530	32		32	783
Chemistry	540	35	5	40	1,326
Geology	550	2	8	10	1,460
Paleontology	560		2	2	80
Biology	570	18	13	31	799
Botany	580	3		3	732
Zoölogy	590	21	2	23	1,694
Useful arts	600	7	6	13	789
Medicine	610	17	4	21	5,382
Engineering	620	3	17	20	909
Agriculture	630	5	10	15	1,176
Domestic economy	640				43
Communication, commerce	650	11	2	13	361
Chemical technology	660	1	2	3	208
Manufactures	670	1	2	3	133
Mechanic trades	680				13
Building	690		1	1	26

Fine arts 700	18	8	26	685
Landscape gardening 710				126
Architecture 720	2	7	9	327
Sculpture 730		4	4	196
Drawing, design, decoration 740		4	4	89
Painting 750	5	62	67	498
Engraving 760				100
Photography 770				77
Music 780	23	1	24	556
Amusements 790	6	2	8	448
Literature 800	54	15	69	1,410
American 810	93	7	100	5,570
English 820	197	7	204	6,541
German 830	170	2	172	3,269
French 840	508	28	536	4,433
Italian 850	21		21	1,055
Spanish 860	10	46	56	458
Latin 870	39	1	40	2,020
Greek 880	37		37	1,765
Minor languages 890	3		3	339
History......................900	27	3	30	1,347
Geography and description 910	55	5	60	5,773
Biography 920	55	31	86	2,728
Ancient history 930	27	2	29	764
Modern history, Europe 940	116	31	147	5,338
Asia 950	6	1	7	251
Africa 960	2		2	109
North America 970	64	14	78	3,070
South America 980		4	4	92
Oceanic and polar regions 990	3		3	97
Alumni collection	2	7	9	1,387
Maine collection	13	40	53	4,599
U. S. Documents (serial set)		17	17	5,869

REPORT OF THE DIRECTOR OF THE MUSEUM OF FINE ARTS

To the President of Bowdoin College:

The Director of the Museum of Fine Arts has the honor to submit the following report for the year ending April 30, 1928:

ACQUISITIONS

May, 1927—Ivory elephant with Chinese enamel pedestal and wooden base; caparisoned with gold harness and howdah set with sapphires and rubies. Height, 17 inches. Given by Mrs. Frank W. Forbes, of Westboro, Mass.

June, 1927—Several impressions from stone tablets; Han Dynasty, about 100 B. C. Given by Mr. Chi-Hai Fong, Class of 1927.

August, 1927—Griechische Vasen Malerei, von Ernst Buschor; Sammlung Göschen-Archäologie, von Professor Dr. Friedrich Koepp, four volumes. Given by Mr. John M. Wulfing, of St. Louis, Mo.

December, 1927—Oil portrait, by William E. Willard, of Chief Justice John Appleton, Class of 1822. Size, 29½ in. x 24½ in. Given by Judge Frederick Hunt Appleton, Class of 1864.

Oil portrait, by William M. Chase, of Mr. William J. Curtis, Class of 1875. Size, 66 in. x 39 in. Given by Mrs. William J. Curtis.

LOANS

January, 1927—A Japanese silver box, with damascened top. Lent by Mr. Harold S. Stetson, Class of 1906.

WITHDRAWALS

August, 1927—An old blue cup and saucer, and a single saucer. Withdrawn by Miss Theodosia Pendleton.

September, 1927—An oil portrait of the Drummond Brothers, by Benjamin West. Withdrawn by Messrs. Scott and Fowles, New York.

April, 1928—Landscape in watercolors, by Sophie Bendelari Markoe. Transferred to the Curator.

EXHIBITIONS

"The Holy Experiment," a portfolio of color plates of the decorations of Violet Oakley in the State Capitol, Harrisburg, Penn., was on exhibition in the Bowdoin Gallery, May 11-19.

A memorial exhibition of thirty-two oil paintings and six watercolors, by the late William Wallace Gilchrist, Jr., lent by private owners and by Mrs. Gilchrist, was held in the Walker Art Building from October 15 to November 5. The exhibition was opened with an evening reception that was well attended by citizens of Brunswick and of some neighboring towns; and during its course was visited by some eight hundred persons.

The "Fifty Great Prints" exhibition organized by the American Federation of Arts came to the Walker Art Building for the month of March; it attracted numerous visitors, especially from the student body of the College.

The New England Conference, American Association of Museums, was held in Portland October 6-8. On the 7th, the Delegates were the guests of Bowdoin College. They were welcomed in the lecture room of the Art Building in an address by President Sills, were shown the museum collections by the Curator, and were served with lunch in the Assyrian Room. In the afternoon they visited the Library, the Chapel, where Professor Wass gave a short organ recital, and the Department of Biology.

The representatives to the State Conference of the Daughters of the American Revolution in Brunswick were given a reception by the College on the evening of March 31, in the Art Building.

At the request of Mr. Edward Perry Warren many objects in his collection of classical antiquities have been photographed during the year, by Mr. G. B. Webber of Brunswick, for the catalogue of the collection which Mr. Warren is preparing.

The gift of the Carnegie Corporation has been installed in Hubbard Hall, in the room on the north of the western corridor now called the Fine Arts Room.

The attendance through the calendar year was 8,650.

Respectfully submitted,

HENRY E. ANDREWS, *Director.*